American Mosaic

American
Mosaic

AFRICAN-AMERICAN CONTRIBUTIONS

The History of African-American Civic Organizations

Joe Ferry

CHELSEA HOUSE
PUBLISHERS
A Haights Cross Communications Company

Philadelphia

Frontis: Brothers of the Alpha Phi Alpha fraternity display their distinctive brands.

CHELSEA HOUSE PUBLISHERS

VP, NEW PRODUCT DEVELOPMENT   Sally Cheney
DIRECTOR OF PRODUCTION   Kim Shinners
CREATIVE MANAGER   Takeshi Takahashi
MANUFACTURING MANAGER   Diann Grasse

Staff for THE HISTORY OF AFRICAN-AMERICAN CIVIC ORGANIZATIONS

ASSOCIATE EDITOR   Benjamin Xavier Kim
PRODUCTION EDITOR   Jaimie Winkler
PICTURE RESEARCHER   PAT HOLL
COVER AND SERIES DESIGNER   Keith Trego
LAYOUT   21st Century Publishing and Communications, Inc.

A Haights Cross Communications ✦ Company

http://www.chelseahouse.com

First Printing

1 3 5 7 9 8 6 4 2

Library of Congress Cataloging-in-Publication Data

Ferry, Joseph.
   The history of African American civic organizations/by
Joe Ferry.
       p. cm.—(American mosaic)
Includes bibliographical references.
   ISBN 0-7910-7270-3 HC
   1. African Americans—Societies, etc.—History. 2. African
Americans—Social conditions. 3. African Americans—Politics
and government. 4. Social classes—United States—History.
5. Elite (Social sciences)—United States—History. I. Title.
II. Series.
E185.5.F47 2003
369'.396073'009—dc21

                                   2003000825

Table of Contents

Boxer Muhammad Ali receiving an award in 1971 from Alpha Phi Alpha. To outsiders, the world of such black organizations as the Boulé, Jack and Jill, or the fraternities and sororities on college campuses seem like a secretive network of prestige and power.

The World of
the Black Elite

The notion of a wealthy upper class among white Americans is a very familiar one, with much literature and history detailing the lives of the old-money families of the Northeast. This aristocracy would look down their noses at the nouveau riche, and their world was inaccessible to the average citizen. One was either born into it, or had to know someone who was already a member.

But it might surprise many to learn that African Americans have had an upper class for at least a hundred years as well. The members of this elite belong to various organizations and make sure their children attend summer camps and join fraternities and sororities with others of their kind. And many of these children themselves grapple with the notion that lighter-colored African Americans are somehow "better" than darker-skinned ones.

The world of the black upper class is a little known or understood layer of the African-American community whose members live on the

7

boundary of two very distinct worlds, never comfortably fitting into either world. It is an awkward situation because members of the black elite are not fully accepted by either the white or black communities. Whites have a tendency to look at them and say, "Well, you don't look like us. You don't have the same heritage as we do, so you're not a part of the group, even if you are well educated and have the money."

But members of the black upper class are also considered outsiders by the black mainstream because they send their kids to places like Camp Atwater, an exclusive black camp that was founded in 1923. They make sure their daughters are presented to society through specific events such as the Links, or the Alpha Kappa Alpha or Delta Sigma Theta cotillions. It is a group that refuses to send its children to public schools, instead embracing certain black boarding schools that were founded at the turn of the century, schools like Palmer Boarding School, and Mather Academy in South Carolina.

One way the black upper class has dealt with its alienation and isolation has been by forming its own social organizations, where like-minded people with similar values can get together for relaxation or to address some of the pressing issues they face. Cathy Lightbourne Connors, one of the most influential society columnists to write for the *New York Amsterdam News*, believes that black social groups serve a valuable role in the country. The media give too much credence to the black urban subculture that has its own language, clothing, and set of values, she says, while ignoring other, more positive aspects of the black community.

"When upper-class and middle-class blacks are kept hidden from the community," said Connors in Lawrence Otis Graham's book *Our Kind of People*, "we fail to produce role models and mentors for young blacks who need to know that there are people like them who still have hope and who have not given up." But Connors also is quick to point out that social groups must recognize that they have to get involved and interact with the people and the local groups they are supposed to be mentoring and helping, instead of being detached while perched in their seat of privilege.

The earliest examples of social organizations were the fraternities and sororities that formed on historically black college campuses. Even though blacks have attended Southern black universities since the 1860s and Northern white universities since the 1800s, black Greek-letter organizations were not established until the early 1900s, more than 125 years after the first white fraternities.

These black college fraternal groups began as small, elite social groups that eventually made scholarly discussion and social activism part of their agenda. When Alpha Phi Alpha, the first black fraternity, was begun by a group of black students at Cornell University in 1906, it was an important bond between the seven black men who belonged, but was virtually invisible to the rest of the mostly white Ithaca, New York campus. But as the presence of Alpha Phi Alpha and the other black fraternities grew on black campuses during the early 1900s, they were each known for building their popularity by seeking out certain desirable student candidates who were smart, accomplished, affluent, athletic, or good-looking. If one didn't have at least one of those qualities, membership was not granted. Even as some campus chapters developed tough standards for minimum grade point averages and other criteria, black Greek life was highly sought after because of the parties and other social gatherings that were offered by fraternity and sorority membership.

Membership in a fraternity or sorority also served another purpose for African-American college students. While there are clearly old-guard black elite who would limit their circle to just those who went to the right black college (Howard, Spelman, Morehouse and Fisk, for example), there are also many others who are willing to expand the circle to include those blacks who went to good white colleges, as long as the good white college experience included membership in one of the black establishment fraternities or sororities.

To understand this mentality is to understand the difference between white fraternity life and black fraternity life. While the former is mostly limited to the three- and four-year college experience, the black fraternity experience begins in college but is an activity that has even greater importance after graduation. It goes far beyond the well-choreographed campus musical "step shows" that the student members present on stage as competitions to show which fraternity can out-step the other with synchronized music and dance steps, and the unique traditions they follow in their attire and speech and actions while "on line."

Fraternities' and sororities' membership create a lasting identity, a circle of lifetime friends, a foundation for future political and community activism. Continuing through their adulthood, membership in a fraternity or sorority often means lifetime subscriptions to publications such as *The Sphinx*, the *Ivy Leaf*, or the *Oracle*. It even means regulated funeral programs with unique services that are specifically outlined for surviving fraternity members in attendance. For many, the black Greek-letter organizations provide a post-college forum through which some of the best-educated blacks in America can discuss an agenda to fight racism and improve conditions for other less-advantaged blacks.

Throughout most of the twentieth century, blacks who attended white colleges were not allowed admission into white fraternities operating on their campuses, just as they were not allowed to live in some of the white housing located on or around their college campuses. Because of this, although five of the first eight black fraternities were founded on black campuses, the black fraternities saw their fastest and widest expansion taking place on white college campuses where black students had no housing and where they were facing extreme discrimination and isolation.

Most blacks who attended historically black colleges had hopes of joining one of the black fraternities because that was one of the

During the '60s, the process of desegregation was a painful one, usually involving the military to help defuse situations such as black students attending classes on campus. This army convoy is shown patrolling the University of Mississippi in 1962 when student James Meredith was the first African American to attend.

surest ways to become accepted among the campus elite. In the early 1900s, the groups were small, intellectually privileged, and rather secretive in their activities.

By the 1930s and 1940s, however, the fraternities and sororities had become more dominant on campus, offering large social gatherings and serving as a magnet for not just the intellectual elite but also the economic elite, who looked at the groups as a way to distinguish themselves from non-members who could not afford the membership fees or pay for the kinds of clothes, parties, and automobiles that were common for members. By the early 1950s, many of the fraternity alumni who stayed active in their graduate chapters had launched important civic programs to respond to the black community and its problems.

While some argued that there was too great a difference between young fraternity members who focused on having a good time and the older fraternity alumni who were using their efforts to advance the black agenda, both groups were often targeted as supporting elite organizations that further divided the larger black community into the privileged and working class.

By the late 1950s, when many of the fraternity members, students as well as alumni, had gotten involved in the Southern civil rights movement, a greater solidarity developed between members and nonmembers. They had a common cause to fight for, whether they were operating on mostly black or mostly white campuses.

A new issue developed for black students who began entering white colleges in the late 1950s and 1960s. Because such bigotry was exhibited by the white Greek-letter organizations on so many campuses where well-to-do, integrated blacks were students, the black Greeks have an even greater role at the white colleges, except at schools like Princeton, where fraternities were not permitted for any racial group.

Barbara Collier Delany's experience at Cornell University in 1956 underscored the problems waiting for black students who faced the white fraternities and sororities operating on white college campuses. Delany made national headlines when, as a student at the Ivy League campus, she was offered membership in the white sorority Sigma Kappa.

Delany was among only a handful of blacks at the college at the time and was the first black offered membership in a white sorority. Delany, who belonged to Jack and Jill, debuted with the Girl Friends, and graduated from Hunter High in Manhattan, said her sorority sisters were nice to her, but officials at the national office were furious that she was being considered for membership. They told the students to reject Delany or face having their chapter shut down.

"When the white students refused to kick me out, headquarters shut down the sorority," said Delany, who still corresponds with some of her classmates.

What helped to make the black fraternities and sororities achieve such a lofty status was their stringent membership requirements that included a high grade point average and extensive community service. To understand the history of the fraternities and sororities of the black elite, it helps to both recognize the reason for their existence and understand the comparisons that are often made between them. Even though fraternity officers have a daily agenda that focuses on developing programs, monitoring legislation, and raising funds to benefit members and their international causes, there is an obvious undercurrent among members that causes these students and past graduates to constantly measure one group against the other.

Unlike whites, who can choose among more than fifty national fraternities and sororities with only a vague sense of how one group differs from others, the black elite has a clear sense of which black fraternities and sororities belong to the National Pan-Hellenic Council, and which ones do not. The NPHC is the governing body of African-American fraternities and sororities.

There are many challenges to the growth of black fraternities and sororities these days. White colleges that have been unsupportive of black fraternities are just one of the challenges that threaten the black Greek system today. The lack of support makes the organizations appear unstable and unpopular, as the groups see their chapters activated, temporarily deactivated, and then reestablished. For example, the Rho Chapter of Delta Sigma Theta was formed at Columbia University in 1923, then deactivated in the 1960s, then reactivated in the 1980s.

Members of the service fraternity Alpha Phi Omega at Howard University. Just as their white counterparts have come under fire for hazing practices, black fraternities have gained notoriety and increased scrutiny for incidents resulting in injury and death at the hands of fraternity brothers.

Another challenge is that black fraternities are not nearly as wealthy as their white counterparts. White frats have generations of rich alumni sending money to build incredible mansions for their frat houses. Black frats and sororities don't have that kind of support because there are so relatively few black alumni with the financial wherewithal to be so generous.

But there are also problems facing some black fraternities that money can't solve. An example is the series of "animal house" type of hazing incidents more typically associated with white Greek-letter organizations. In recent years there have been a rising number of violent incidents during the admissions or initiation stages at several campus chapters. In 1994, for example, at Southeast Missouri State in Cae Girardeau, a student pledge of Kappa Alpha Psi died from injuries inflicted by two frat brothers who later pleaded guilty to involuntary manslaughter.

In 1995, a University of Maryland student sued Omega Psi Phi and was awarded $375,000 after he suffered injuries following initiation beatings that lasted over a four-week period. The student, Joseph Snell, said that frat brothers regularly hit him with a hammer and a horsewhip, and that they forced an electric space heater near his face in order to darken his skin because they felt he wasn't black enough.

The National Pan-Hellenic Council has since come out in opposition to hazing and has threated to revoke the membership of any fraternity or sorority that does not prohibit "physical, mental or verbal abuse, scare tactics, horseplay, practical jokes or tricks, and any humiliating or demeaning acts" as a prerequisite for membership.

Debbie Allen, left, and Phylicia Rashad at the 73rd Annual Academy Awards in 2001. These two women are members of the Jack and Jill organization, one of the largest groups in the world and one that involves children of members and encourages them to mix with other similarly privileged children through summer camps and other activities.

2

Jack and Jill
of America, Inc.

When Marion Turner Stubbs Thomas first invited twenty women friends to a meeting in her Philadelphia home on January 24, 1938, she probably didn't realize the incredible impact her action would have for generations to come.

Thomas, a concert pianist and mother, envisioned a social club that would connect her children with others from local black families. She hoped to rally the visiting mothers to help provide cultural opportunities that the Great Depression and Jim Crow laws had denied to most young African Americans.

From those humble beginnings, Jack and Jill of America, Inc. has grown into an international force of almost 40,000 mothers, fathers and children with 220 chapters across the United States and the Republic of Germany. A nonprofit service organization, it focuses on bringing together African-American children and introducing them to various educational, social and cultural experiences. In addition to sponsoring public service projects in their communities, the various Jack and Jill chapters raise money for local nursing homes, shelters, hospitals and educational institutions. What started as a simple idea born of friendship and necessity became one of the country's most prestigious service organizations for black families.

The membership and alumni roster of Jack and Jill reads like a page from Who's Who Among Black Americans: Alma Brown, celebrity sisters Phylicia Rashad and Debbie Allen, and the late Betty Shabbazz are just a few of the more prominent members. But like the figures in the organization's namesake nursery rhyme, members of Jack and Jill of America have discovered they must climb new hills to meet the challenges of the future.

National president Sheryl Benning Thomas believes Jack and Jill must not only continue its traditions of support of children's rights issues, education, and community service ethics in youngsters, but must also evolve to meet the needs of the times. A change made a few years ago in the organization's bylaws, for example, made it possible for the organization to expand its membership to more than one club per city, which should help spur growth.

"The expansion of Jack and Jill is happening quickly," Thomas said. "We've opened the door for new interest groups to start."

Along with expanding Jack and Jill, vice president Sylvia McGee said one of the main goals of the organization is to continue producing generations of new leaders.

Although membership in Jack and Jill is open to mothers by invitation only, husbands and fathers have been involved in the work of the organization from the beginning. They have served as mentors, fund-raisers and chaperones. McGee and other members believe the time has come to define their role and make it a more permanent part of the institution.

In 1997, Jack and Jill officially kicked off its fathers' auxiliary with the election of national chair Fitzroy Younge. McGee said that innovation speaks to the needs of today's children.

"Sixty years ago, you had two-parent families intact, but even in Jack and Jill we have a lot of single-parent families," McGee said. "All children need a male presence, so now they can get those positive role models through Jack and Jill."

The same year, on the grounds of the Oak Brook Hills Hotel and Resort outside Chicago, the organization took another step up the hill toward its future by convening its first national teen summit. Along with leadership workshops, participants drafted their own bylaws and discussed their vision for the next century. "We can use technology to bring Jack and Jill into the future," said Brian Delaney, a sixteen-year-old from Englewood, California, who attended the summit.

Delaney used his knowledge of computers to create a web page for the Far West region, where he was president. Others got more involved in affecting legislation concerning children and changing the image some have of Jack and Jill as an organization removed from the interests of the black community at large.

"Either they don't know anything about us or they see Jack and Jill as a bunch of rich, upper-class blacks who are staying amongst themselves and not giving back to the community," said Courtney Wesley, who was South Central regional teen president.

Growing up, Wesley recalled the Jack and Jill-sponsored mixers and the socials she attended, but also the holidays spent at community centers and homeless shelters, and reading stories at churches to preschoolers. It's important for people to know about the volunteer work Jack and Jill performs, she said.

The service component of the organization evolved over the years. Back in 1938 when Jack and Jill was founded, there were more social gatherings and networking. The Philadelphia chapter, for example, planned Halloween parties for the children, trips to see local plays, and times for storytelling and music appreciation.

News of the fledgling club traveled fast. The first members "gathered people that they knew—their friends, people in their churches, in their sororities, in their communities," said Thomas. "That was the nucleus of Jack and Jill."

Momentum spread quickly to other eastern cities such as New York City, Pittsburgh, and Boston, where members used their swelling numbers to make positive changes in the black community. As early as the 1940s, the group started national service projects such as research for rheumatic fever, volunteering for local agencies and efforts to end segregation.

"Members branched out from a small tea-set mentality and providing opportunities for their children to providing them for people in the communities," Thomas said.

In later years, Jack and Jill worked toward more of a balance between service and social activities. Members adopted foster homes and hospices and sent care packages to African nations. They raised money for polio research. In 1968, the organization officially added a fund-raising arm to its governing body—the Jack and Jill of America Foundation Inc.

Thomas' personal memories of Jack and Jill are from her hometown of Cleveland, Ohio. For a few years, her mother was local president. Thomas didn't appreciate the full potential of the club when she was young. "I saw it as a social group. I didn't see the service," she admitted.

Thomas considers herself a child of the Civil Rights movement. She marched with Dr. Martin Luther King Jr. and attended nonviolent protests. But when she became a mother, she found herself fondly remembering her experiences in Jack and Jill.

"I wanted to find a group with the same goals I had for myself and my children," Thomas said. "I knew Jack and Jill would provide cultural and educational activities for them. So I saw Jack and Jill in my life as being important."

Through Jack and Jill, the Detroit elementary school principal found a way to blend her politics with her passions—advocating for the rights of her children and others. In recent years, Jack and Jill members have attended Stand for Children, a national rally called by Children's Defense Fund President Marian Wright Edelman.

Marian Wright Edelman, the organizer of the rally Stand for Children, a cause that Jack and Jill members have supported, along with other civic improvement projects. The work that they accomplish is rarely trumpeted in the media, as Jack and Jill do not seek widespread recognition.

They have written letters protesting the Republican Contract with America and funded international projects such as building a well in Mali and a school in the Gambia.

Currently, the organization is working to build awareness

of health needs among African Americans. Chapters hold health fairs and poster contests and join a walkathon with the Links organization.

"What I really love about Jack and Jill is that it instills in your children that service is part of your life," Thomas said. "They just take it for granted."

The club is open to children aged two and one half to nineteen. Alumni groups also have formed on the campuses of historically black colleges and universities. From the youngest to the oldest, children learn that community service is not an option. It's expected of them, Thomas said. Toddlers and preschoolers bake brownies for senior citizen homes. Preteens serve meals to the homeless. High school students have helped build homes with Habitat for Humanity.

Teens like Courtney Wesley and Brian Delaney said that lasting friendships form through those experiences. Those bonds are strengthened when they see each other again on college campuses. Almost all Jack and Jill alumni attend college.

For more than sixty years, the organization has labored quietly in the shadows, preferring to let its actions speak volumes. It doesn't beat its own drum in the media. Members are quiet about what they do, trying to improve conditions in the community for their own and for others. That is their source of joy and satisfaction.

When she founded Jack and Jill, Marion Turner Stubbs Thomas had the same concerns for her children as did other well-to-do black women who saw their children growing up during a period when blacks had access to few positive black images and to few activities that brought them into contact with other middle- and upper-class black families.

The daughter of Dr. John P. Turner, a surgeon who was the first black on Philadelphia's Board of Education, Marion was born in Philadelphia and graduated from the University of Pennsylvania in 1930. A child of affluent and worldly parents, she attended the Sorbonne in France, then returned to the

United States and married a thoracic surgeon, Frederick Douglas Stubbs, in 1934.

After Stubbs died, Marion married Detroit physician Alf Thomas, and the two became a celebrated couple among that city's black elite. They raised three daughters in Jack and Jill, all of whom went on to raise their own children in the organization as well.

The other women in the Jack and Jill organizing chapter in 1938 came from affluent families as well. Among them was Helen Dickens, a physician who later became a professor and associate dean at the University of Pennsylvania School of Medicine; Sadie T. M. Alexander, an attorney who had earned a Ph.D. from the University of Pennsylvania in 1921 and whose husband, Raymond Pace Alexander, was a Philadelphia judge; and Dorothy Wright, who was married to Emanuel Crogman Wright, son of the founder of the Citizens and Southern Bank and Trust Company.

Dorothy Wright, who was also pivotal in the later creation of the elite black women's group, the Links, was the first national president of Jack and Jill.

"One of the major reasons why parents want their kids to grow up in Jack and Jill is the social and education benefits," said Shirley Barber, the group's fifteenth national president. "Even if you send your children to the best private schools and colleges, it doesn't mean that they will get to meet black role models who inspire them and make them feel that they can succeed in a white world. That's what Jack and Jill can do."

Because Jack and Jill is very selective and admits members by invitation only, it provides a great opportunity for professional parents to introduce their kids to children of similar families. Whether in Boston, Atlanta, Houston or Beverly Hills, the children of a community's most prominent black families will be found as members of the local Jack and Jill chapter. For generations, it has served as a network for parents who want playgroups for their children, as well as a network for young adults who want companionship, dating relationships, and, ultimately, marriage partners.

William Pickens, who was first enrolled in Jack and Jill as a two-year-old in 1938, said he wasn't surprised that he eventually married a girl who grew up in Jack and Jill. His parents wanted him and his brother in the organization so they would be introduced to other black kids who came from similar backgrounds, he recalled.

Pickens, whose father, William, was a lawyer and whose mother, Emilie, was national president of the group in the early 1950s, came from the kind of family background for which Jack and Jill has become known. Pickens' father was a classmate of poet Langston Hughes at Lincoln University in Pennsylvania, and his grandfather, a 1904 graduate of Yale University, was the first black dean of Morgan State University. His mother graduated from the University of Washington in 1923 and was a descendant of one of the oldest black families in Pennsylvania.

Pickens, who went on to serve as president of the Paul Robeson Foundation in New York, recalled that many of his friendships, as well as his marriage, grew out of ties to Jack and Jill. His wife, Audrey Brannen Pickens, had been a teen president of her chapter in Queens, New York. He had been social chairman of his New York chapter. The Jack and Jill tradition continued for Pickens' three children and grandchildren.

"We had a lot in common," Pickens said of his upbringing in Jack and Jill. "Like many kids in the group, we grew up spending our summers in Sag Harbor and going to the same cotillions."

According to Lawrence Otis Graham, most of the kids who grew up with him in Jack and Jill lived an almost completely white existence during the week. Unlike most of their parents, who had grown up in segregated towns and school systems with black neighbors and teachers, Graham and his friends lived in all-white neighborhoods and attended classes with white students who had never seen a black face—other than those of the

Jack and Jill member Alma Brown, right, with son Michael Brown. Brown is the widow of former U.S. Secretary of Commerce Ron Brown, another example of Jack and Jill's connections to high-level positions.

custodians. They played with white kids who claimed them as their "favorite" black friend. In fact, their Monday through Friday school experience was so well-integrated that they rarely heard racial discussions outside the house.

As Graham himself writes:

But when Saturday came, there was a collective sigh of relief as we could remove the masks and settle into our black upper-class reality. We had our Jack and Jill gatherings: carpools of black mothers and fathers pulling up to museums or riding stables in Ford and Buick station wagons, or groups of kids getting off a plane in order to visit our congressmen in Washington. No matter how different all of our weekend activities were, we were around other black kids, where we black children could be ourselves and tell each other exactly what we thought. We could talk about racist incidents just the way way we talked about baseball and coin collecting. We could talk about how we were sick of all the *What's Happening!!* ghetto dwellers on TV while also talking about some new remote-control airplane we were building at home.

While the organization operates with local chapters or branches, a national office actually controls Jack and Jill, with each local chapter chartered under the group's constitution and bylaws. Each chapter, in turn, is broken down into special age groups consisting of toddlers aged two to four; young children aged five to eight; preteens ages nine to 11; junior teens, who are 12 to 14; and senior teens, who are in high school.

Age-appropriate activities are provided for each of the different groups. The parents and officers—usually the mothers, although fathers are allowed to participate—chaperone their child's groups to museums, theater performances, sporting events and overnight trips to historic places in the United States and abroad. There is an activity at least once a month and there is often a focus on learning about black history.

Depending on the size of each chapter's separate age groups, monthly organizing meetings are held at members' homes or at local clubs or hotels. During the year, there are usually two or three parties just for the kids, at least two being formal or semi-formal. And at least twice a year there will be a semiformal or formal party given at a private club or hotel just for the parents and their invited guests. Many of the Jack and Jill chapters also sponsor debutante cotillions for those young girls who have reached their senior year in high school and who will simultaneously graduate from their chapters.

Regardless of their age, members get a heavy dose of tradition and organizational history. At local conferences there are always photo displays of past officers. At national conventions, there are always speeches by officers. Knowing who started the group and why is something members are required to know and remember.

The exclusive membership in Jack and Jill is frustrating for some parents, especially wealthy professionals who are accustomed to paying for any house, car or summer camp they want. Membership, unfortunately, is not for sale. Parents covet it because they know the organization will provide their children and themselves with a network of activities and friendship that will last a lifetime.

The way to get into Jack and Jill is to know someone who is already a member. But it is much more complicated than that. After a current member sponsors a candidate, no interview can take place unless there is a spot open for a new family to join. In fact, the only people guaranteed admission to Jack and Jill are those whose parents were in the organization as children.

Wanting to get in and getting in are two different things. There is no minimum family income threshold required of those being considered for membership. But because members are required to entertain fellow chapter members in their homes in between larger events that take place at country clubs, hotels and restaurants, it is no surprise that the most successful applicants are the ones who have the space, the money, and the time to entertain and host parties.

The impressive résumés of the organization's past presidents demonstrate to local chapter members and others that professional accomplishments are crucial to Jack and Jill's success. Almost all past presidents had been members of the exclusive Links group as well as Delta Sigma Theta or Alpha Kappa Alpha—long considered the choice college sororities of the black elite. As Nellie Gordon Roulhac's history book on Jack and Jill, *The First Fifty Years*, reveals, many of the women held doctorates in medicine or teaching and most were members of prominent families.

For example, Dorothy Bell Wright, the group's first president, was an accountant with the Internal Revenue Service. Her great-grandfather, Private John Henson Swails, joined the Union Army in 1864. Her husband's family had founded one of the most respected black banks in the country. Dorothy's daughter, Gwynne Wright, grew up in a home where famous names and faces were always passing through.

Emilie Pickens, the second president of the group, was descended from Jack Montier, a Philadelphia resident who appeared in Benjamin Franklin's 1790 census and built a historic home that has stood since the 1770s. A 1923 graduate of the University of Washington, she was married to a successful attorney. Her son, Bill, still visits with Jack and Jill kids he met in the late 1930s and 1940s. "Most of my oldest friends are the children of the Jack and Jill mothers that my mom worked with," said Pickens, who was living in New York City at the time.

Other early national presidents of Jack and Jill attracted intellectual prestige, a quality that brought depth to the group. The next three presidents—Alberta Banner Turner, Nellie Gordon Roulhac, and Ruth Brown Howard—all held doctorates. Turner had been the first black to earn a Ph.D. in psychology from Ohio State University before serving as professor of psychology at several universities, including Wilberforce and Lincoln. Roulhac, who sat on the board of directors of the United Cerebral Palsy Association, had earned masters and doctorate degrees from Columbia University and the University of Sarasota. She was the child of an old Philadelphia family, and her father and grandfather also held doctorates. Her successor, Ruth Howard, was a graduate of Wellesley and Columbia and received her Ph.D. from Catholic University before writing several college textbooks and joining the faculty of San Francisco State University.

The leadership's progression from social elite to intellectual elite and then to professional elite was evident by the late 1960s. Ninth and tenth presidents Miriam Chivers Shropshire and Pearl Boschulte, both graduates of Howard Medical School,

Dr. Betty Shabazz, widow of Malcolm X, who was another member of Jack and Jill. However, the organization has not taken any public stands on controversial issues in the way the NAACP or other similar organizations have.

were physicians who practiced internal medicine and ophthalmology, respectively.

Others like Lillian Adams Park, Margaret Simms, Eleanor DeLoache Brown, Ramona Arnold, Nellie Thornton, Shirley

Barber James, and Eva Wanton, were all educators with masters' degrees or Ph.D.s. Not surprisingly, most of them were also members of other black groups such as the Links, as well as predominantly white groups such as the Junior League.

The credentials of the people that have been running this organization can be unique and quite intimidating to prospective members. The families that belong to the organization and the mothers that hold the offices reflect a unique mix of black and white social credentials and political activism. They represent the very best that black America has to offer, a great standard to set for kids who are looking for role models.

Each year, the organization publishes an annual yearbook called "Up the Hill," which features photos and reports from local chapters as they detail their service, cultural, and social activities of the prior year. The pink and blue book is as a thick as a big city telephone directory and serves as a chronicle of growing up in the black elite, coast to coast. Many think of its as a black children's version of the Social Register. Although Jack and Jill's earliest chapters began in urban areas similar to Philadelphia and New York City, the greater trend today is toward developing chapters within suburban communities where black parents are hard-pressed to find black friendships for their children, who are reaching a crucial stage of social development in their lives.

Interracial dating is still an uncomfortable issue for even the most open-minded black families. Many black families living in predominantly white neighborhoods point to the fast-growing chapters in suburban communities as a means of addressing the conflicts of interracial dating. For some, it is a means of avoiding interracial dating.

"I got so tired of hearing my friends tell me about their older black sons, boys from good families, who were bringing home these white girlfriends from school because they supposedly didn't know any well-bred black girls," said a woman who had just returned from a teen summit in Oklahoma City. "I got busy and put my son in Jack and Jill. I know it sounds desperate, but it was the best move I could make to let him know that there are black girls who are smart, attractive, well to do, and well bred. In Jack and Jill, we've got debutantes, intellectuals, athletes, politicos, artists, everything you could imagine."

Since it is not a political organization, Jack and Jill has never taken a public stand on controversial issues such as interracial relationships in ways that groups like the National Association for the Advancement of Colored People (NAACP) or the Association of Black Social Workers have. Many members do say that if the group is going to see any changes in the near future, it will be in deciding how far it will go to address the needs and concerns of the interracial family.

In the early years, Jack and Jill, like many groups that catered to the black establishment in the first half of the twentieth century, attracted a negative reaction from many blacks who lacked the resources, the upbringing, or the physical appearance to be considered for membership. History shows that some chapters, particularly those in larger Southern cities, were guilty of placing a great emphasis on these characteristics. But others were unfairly attacked for doing the same thing when what really was happening was that they were just nominating people who were in their social circle, their church, their bridge club. And not surprisingly, these darker, less-pedigreed people had long been shut out of these institutions.

Today, Jack and Jill continues to take its goals and objectives seriously. Through bold new steps, it is raising awareness of children's needs and concerns in black communities, and doing something about them. Through national incentives such as the "Million Point Health Plan" and through collaboration with organizations such as the Links and Children's Defense Foundation, Jack and Jill chapters across the nation are making a difference in the lives of their families and those in the communities they serve.

An Alpha Phi Alpha paddle in the foreground at the Greek Picnic festival held annually in Philadelphia. Alpha Phi Alpha is the oldest African-American fraternity, and was founded at Cornell University in 1906.

3

Greek Brotherhood

African-American fraternities developed, in large part, because of the alienation and isolation black college students were feeling at the time. The turn of the century was an especially abusive and oppressive time for African Americans, one rife with racial inequality and social disadvantage.

In 1896, for example, the Supreme Court ruled through its *Plessy vs. Ferguson* decision that separate facilities for black and whites were permissible under the Constitution. Segregation or "Jim Crow" laws were prevalent throughout the country—both in the South, with its strict and visible segregation, and in the North, where discrimination occurred in more subtle ways. The late 1800s also saw African-American leader Booker T. Washington offer his infamous "Southern Compromise," in which he stated that in all things social, African Americans and whites could be separate "as the fingers on my hand."

The situation facing African Americans on the Cornell University campus at the time was similar to what was playing out in society at large. Blacks were isolated and segregated from the general student population. The result was a horrendous retention rate for black students in college. Six African-American students who attended Cornell in 1904-05 did not return the following year. Worried about the dwindling black student body, a group of African Americans created a study and support group for remaining black students on campus.

Secret societies in 1906 provided the support system for white students at Cornell. In addition to the advantage of finding students of common backgrounds and interest, fraternities and sororities provided housing, study groups, and a social environment in which to grow with others. But, because black students were excluded from these secret societies, there was nowhere for them to turn except to each other. With the success of the study group during the 1905-06 year, the black students began exploring ways to make the group more purposeful and permanent. One of the ideas raised was to form a fraternity.

On December 4, 1906, seven black students on the Cornell University campus decided to form an organization for which there had been no predecessor. They became the founders of the first African-American fraternity in the United States. Alpha Phi Alpha is the oldest of all the black Greek-letter college organizations. It was the only black fraternity or sorority to have been started at an Ivy League school. The men—Henry Arthur Callis, Eugene Kinckle Jones, Robert Harold Ogle, Charles Henry Chapman, Nathaniel Allison Murray, George Biddle Kelly, and Vertner Woodson Tandy—became known as the "Seven Jewels of the Alpha Phi Alpha Fraternity."

As Alpha Phi Alpha spread from campus to campus, it became clear to the Seven Jewels that their organization was becoming quite powerful. But maintaining communications among chapters was difficult. With that in mind they formed *The Sphinx*, the second oldest African-American national magazine and the fraternity's link around the country. With it, brothers have been able to keep track of fraternity business, provide information on social activities, and write essays on the important issues of the time. Another way the fraternity bridged the communications gap has been by hosting annual conventions. These meetings not only set policy for the fraternity, but also secure and strengthen the fraternal bonds between brothers.

Identifying themselves with programs that emphasized scholarship rather than mere social interaction, the Alphas in 1919 launched a national "Go to High School, Go To College" campaign to combat the eighth-grade dropout rate of 90 percent among black children. The success of that program prompted the Alphas to take on other community service projects, including a voting rights program. Under the phrase "A Voteless People is a Hopeless People," Alpha launched a voter registration drive at a time when voting rights were not guaranteed to African Americans.

In 1935, the Alphas also contributed resources and manpower to assist in the racial discrimination suit by black Amherst College graduate Donald Murray, who had been rejected by the University of Maryland Law School because he was not white. Not only did the fraternity pay his school expenses, but the group also provided his attorneys, who were Alphas and well-known civil rights attorneys: Thurgood Marshall and Charles Hamilton Houston. The fraternity also gave support to a case that successfully challenged the practices of segregation at the University of Texas Law School when Alpha brother Herman Sweatt applied.

The period after World War II represented a time of dynamic activism for the fraternity. In the previous decades, Alpha brothers had been establishing themselves as the leaders of the African-American community. As they were becoming educators, doctors, lawyers, and other community leaders, Alphas became dissatisfied with the overall plight of the African-American community. With its strong financial support of the National Association for the Advancement of

Colored People, Alpha spent the 1950s on the frontline of the civil rights movement.

The leadership and support of individual Alpha men as well as the national organization helped to shape the rise of Dr. Martin Luther King Jr. and the civil rights movement in America. As an Alpha brother, Dr. King was able to rely on fraternity members to organize marches, rallies, and fund-raisers for the movement. In 1955, Dr. King received the Alpha Man of the Year award for his efforts in the Montgomery Bus Boycott.

Today, Alpha Phi Alpha has more than 150,000 members, with 750 chapters scattered across the United States, Africa, Asia, Europe and the Caribbean. Working with the support of a $400,000 grant from the W. K. Kellogg Foundation, the fraternity operates mentoring centers in fifteen major cities around the United States that serve as after-school sites for inner-city teenagers.

Alpha has formed national mentoring partnerships with organizations dedicated to helping minority youth, such as Big Brothers/Big Sisters of America, Boy Scouts of America, March of Dimes and the Head Start program. The fraternity is also involved with Habitat for Humanity to construct decent and affordable housing for the needy.

The membership of Alpha Phi Alpha has included such notables as Marshall, who went to become a Supreme Court Justice, and Dr. King; Atlanta mayors Andrew Young and Maynard Jackson; scholar W.E.B. DuBois; former Congressman William Gray, who went on to head the United Negro College Fund; Olympic gold medallist Jesse Owens; and New York City mayor David Dinkins.

Another popular fraternity for black men—and a strong rival for Alpha—is Omega Psi Phi. It is often thought of as the fraternity with the most personality and the most gregarious members. The branding tradition, shared by other African-American fraternities, is most closely associated with the Omegas. Usually referred to as the "Q's," many new members of the Omega have been branded on the arm with a hot iron

Former Alpha Phi Alpha brother Thurgood Marshall was the first African American to be nominated to the Supreme Court. He was subsequently appointed as a Justice, capping off a remarkable legal career.

displaying the fraternity's letters. While others have tried this painful procedure, the Omegas were most famous for it because the practice played into the group's more macho reputation. Further highlighting that image is the Omegas' secret rally cry, a barking sound that young frat brothers will often make at large Omega gatherings.

Like most other black Greek-letter organizations, Omega Psi Phi was founded at Howard University. In 1911, three students—Edgar Love, Frank Coleman, and Oscar Cooper—formed the fraternity with the help of biology professor Dr. Ernest Just, a black Dartmouth graduate who also earned a doctorate from the University of Chicago.

A chapter of Alpha Phi Alpha already existed on the Howard University campus. But the four organizers felt the time had come for an African-American fraternity to be founded on an African-American campus. A key question facing the founders was the new fraternity's mission. What would it stand for? Both Love and Cooper realized the fraternity would need dynamic leaders who served the African-American community. They would have to be united and committed to their ideals.

On Friday evening November 17, 1911, the three liberal arts students with the help of Just, their faculty advisor, founded the Omega Psi Phi fraternity. Most Omegas are quick to point out proudly that Just is the only fraternity founder to appear on a U.S. postage stamp.

The motto of Omega Psi Phi is "Friendship is essential to the soul." The founders agreed the fraternity would be based on four guiding principles: scholarship, manhood, perseverance, and uplift.

After selecting charter members and drafting a constitution, the men submitted their new organization for recognition by the Howard University administration. It was not an easy task. The Howard administration—and other colleges at the time—was discouraging the formation of fraternities and sororities. They were afraid that secret societies developed a lack of trust among the student body and could be a channel for a lack of morality.

At first, the administration refused to honor the request in a timely manner. Undaunted, the brothers undertook a massive publicity and public relations campaign on campus. They placed index cards announcing their presence on trees, fences, bulletin boards and anywhere else they could think of to be visible to the student body and administration. The administration was not happy about the tactics, but the student body became excited. When the administration refused to give in, the founders turned to plan B: personal lobbying of the faculty.

Still, the administration was slow to recognize Omega. In 1912, the administration postponed a decision on the fraternity and sought more data about Greek organization in general at various universities. Disappointed, the Omegas moved forward, voting in another class of members and, for the first time, taking an oath of allegiance.

For the next two years, Omega made slow progress with the faculty and administration. Finally, in 1914, the fraternity became incorporated, completing its birth and setting the stage for national expansion. Consisting of a large number of physicians and dentists, the group has grown to a membership of approximately 130,000, with more than 700 chapters around the world. Among the Omega membership are Virginia governor L. Douglas Wilder; Atlanta mayor Bill Campbell; Urban League head Vernon Jordan; Howard professor Charles Drew; former NAACP heads Roy Wilkins and Benjamin Hooks; actor and comedian Bill Cosby; Reverend Jesse Jackson; and poet Langston Hughes.

Like Alpha Phi Alpha, Omega Psi Phi has played an active role in the civil rights movement. Omega brothers were active in sit-ins and other demonstrations designed to call attention to the plight of African Americans.

"Operation Big Vote" was successful in getting thousands of black people to vote in the 1976 election. At about the same time, the fraternity made a $250,000 contribution to the United Negro College Fund and pledged an annual gift of $50,000 in perpetuity to the organization.

Although equally respected with Alpha and Omega, the fraternity that is least identified with a particular stereotype is Kappa Alpha Psi. It is also the smallest of the three old-guard fraternities.

Founded at Indiana University in Bloomington, Indiana, with

only ten black students on campus, Kappa Alpha Nu was incorporated as a national fraternity on May 15, 1911. Its tenets were Christian ideals and a purpose of achievement.

Three years later, the fraternity changed its name to Kappa Alpha Psi. One of the reasons for the change may have been a racist comment made by a white Indiana University student, who referred to a brother as a member of "Kappa Alpha Nig."

Between 1914 and 1918, the fraternity expanded rapidly, establishing chapters between the Atlantic and the Pacific. After World War I, the organization consolidated and new alumni chapters formed. With an increase in the number of applicants, Kappa Alpha Psi created the Scroller Club, which helped unify a pledge program. The *Kappa Alpha Psi Journal* became a monthly publication in 1921.

Kappa's first national service program was known as the "Guide Right" program. Its purpose was to help high school seniors in their constant strive for achievement through chapel programs, tutorial services, and meetings and lectures for young students. An outgrowth of Guide Right was the Kappa Instructional Leadership League, or Kappa League, as it is more commonly called. Created in the 1960s by Los Angeles Kappas, it is designed to help young men develop critical leadership skills in whatever field they choose. The program is divided into such categories as self-identity, training, competition, social, and health education. The program was so successful that it became a model for other Kappa chapters throughout the country to follow.

The Kappa Alpha Psi Foundation, created in 1981, has the simple function of raising funds and making grants for undergraduate housing, endowments, scholarships, and other programs. In more than twenty years, Kappa brothers have raised more than $300,000 for the Foundation.   During the 1970s and 1980s, Kappa Alpha Psi worked on a number of social fronts. The fraternity became a member of the Leadership Conference on Civil Rights, a coalition of organizations dedicated to establishing full and equal

A member of Kappa Alpha Psi wearing his letters at the Greek Picnic in Philadelphia. The fraternity was originally founded at Indiana University in Bloomington, Indiana, in 1911 as Kappa Alpha Nu.

rights for all Americans. Within the organization, Kappa was able to oppose congressional bills such as the Equal Educational Opportunities Act of 1972, which was an obvious attempt to undermine busing and civil rights.

Kappa individuals also have played key roles in bringing about social change. The Reverend Leon Sullivan, who became the first African-American board member of General Motors Corporation, made great use of his position. He was successful in mobilizing

American protest of the racist South African regime, while setting standards of conduct for American companies doing business in South Africa.

The 1990s brought about significant change for Kappa. The fraternity took a hard look at its pledge process and decided it needed to be restructured. The fraternity decided to return to methods more closely identified with early membership requirements envisioned by the founders. The purpose was to lessen the incidences of hazing during pledge activities.

One of the most significant accomplishments for Kappa during the 1990s was construction of a new International Headquarters. Kappa had occupied the same building in Philadelphia since 1952, and there was an obvious need for change. In 1989, the process began and two years later, on July 6, 1991, with more than 1,000 Kappamen attending, the new building on North Broad Street in Philadelphia was dedicated.

Today, Kappa Alpha Psi consists of approximately 110,000 members in about 660 chapters. While the Alphas and Omegas often find themselves paired off with the Alpha Kappa Alpha and Delta Sigma Theta sororities, the Kappas are not officially associated with one of the sororities. Although they have annual conventions, the Kappas also gather every two years at assemblies to elect a new Grand Polemarch, the highest-ranking Kappa officer. Among the most well-known Kappas are New York attorney and businessman Percy Sutton, Congressman John Conyers, former Urban League head John Jacob, and former Los Angeles mayor Tom Bradley.

The fourth predominantly African-American fraternity formed soon after the turn of the twentieth century was Phi Beta Sigma. A. Langston Taylor, Leonard Morse, and Charles I. Brown officially founded the fraternity in 1914 at Howard University. The founders met in Morse's house in November 1913 to initiate their first nine members into the new organization. They met again two months later at a Washington, D.C., YMCA and left with a new motto: "Culture for Service and Service for Humanity." Taylor was elected first national president of the fraternity.

By the 1920s, Phi Beta Sigma had added forty five chapters in twenty five American cities. The fraternity served an activist role by supporting antilynching laws and showing interest in international issues such as conditions in the Republic of Haiti. Many African Americans felt U.S. intervention in Haitian affairs was wrong and the fraternity took a stand against it.

During the 1920s, Phi Beta Sigma launched a national program called "Bigger and Better Business." The fraternity was one of the first organizations to realize that economic power was a key component in the empowerment of the African-American community. The program came about after a Sigma brother bought merchandise in large quantities and at a substantial discount for the Colored Merchants Associated. Although the CMA later disbanded, the fraternity realized the potential and created "Bigger and Better." The program helped the image of African-American fraternities, which were thought by critics to be either frivolous or dangerous. "Bigger and Better" was a program that appealed to a broad constituency. With 650 chapters, the Washington, D.C.-based fraternity often partners with its sister organization, Zeta Phi Beta, on civic projects such as voter registration among blacks, and Project SATAP (Sigmas Against Teenage Pregnancy), a program aimed at reducing teen pregnancy.

Although its membership has included Dr. George Washington Carver, Atlanta builder Herman Russell, Chicago Mayor Harold Washington and Congressman John Lewis, the group has never enjoyed the same prestige as the Alphas, Omegas and Kappas.

The youngest and smallest of the major African-American fraternities is Iota Phi Theta. It was founded in 1963, a turbulent year for African Americans with the civil rights movement in full swing. As America moved in a new direction, African-American students (and youth in general) became increasingly dissatisfied by their situation. No longer willing to accept traditional organization membership, many formed their own groups. One was the Student Non-Violent Coordinating Committee, which was instrumental in mobilizing African-American students and youth in the South. The Black Panthers also formed, as many militant African-American youth began demanding freedom immediately, not for the future.

It was against this backdrop, on the campus of Morgan State College in Baltimore, Maryland, that the Iota Phi Theta Fraternity was born, encompassing all the aspirations and ideals of the new emerging feelings in African America. The twelve founders represented a new type of student on the American campus. Each was three to five years older than his peers. Some had wives and children. Others had spent time in the military. And they all had full-time jobs in addition to their studies. Most of the founders had known each other for many years. Combined with their overall maturity, it provided a different outlook on what a fraternity should be all about.

For the founders of Iota Phi Theta, being part of a fraternity meant that hazing pledges was not only destructive but also immoral, especially during a time when black men were dying in the streets for civil rights. They also believed that a modern fraternity should not rely on outdated methods of outreach to the community. To the founders, the purpose of the fraternity was to encourage the development and continuation of scholarship, leadership, citizenship, fidelity, and brotherhood among men. Its spirit is best summarized by its motto: "Building on a Tradition, Not Resting on One."

Between 1963 and 1967, the fraternity experienced typical growing pains. Since most members were older students who lived off-campus, recruiting new brothers was difficult. Another obstacle was that Iota was not represented as a member of the National Pan-Hellenic Council, the governing body of African-American fraternities and sororities. While Iota distinguished itself at Morgan State with high grade point averages and student leadership, its exclusion from the NPHC hurt recruiting.

The Iota Phi Theta fraternity was founded in 1963 at Morgan State College in Baltimore, Maryland. As a relatively new fraternity, Iota Phi Theta's founders were not bound by traditions usually held by older fraternities, and felt that hazing was a detrimental and immoral policy.

Students at Morgan State and elsewhere looked to NPHC membership as a sort of validation for fraternities and sororities. Iota remained small and local until 1967 when a group known as the "Pied Pipers" pledged the fraternity. The Pied Pipers took it upon themselves to spread the Iota philosophy throughout colleges up and down the Eastern Seaboard. It would change the face and scope of Iota forever.

Since the beginning of the fraternity, Iota members have striven to be at the forefront of African-American issues. One of its first acts of defiance was the boycott of a segregated shopping center in Baltimore. This led to other cooperative efforts designed to help the African-American community. During the 1960s and

1970s, Iotas worked on behalf of the Big Brothers of America organization. The fraternity also has worked with the NAACP, the United Negro College Fund, the Southern Christian Leadership Conference, Project IMAGE, the National Federation of the Blind, and the National Sickle Cell Foundation.

In 1993, the fraternity created two important national initiatives that remain as the primary focus of its community service: The National Iota Foundation and the Iota Youth Alliance. The foundation is a nonprofit, tax-exempt organization that serves as a clearinghouse for funding and programs for worthwhile endeavors. Since its creation, the foundation and its subsidiaries have distributed more than $250,000 in grants, aid, and services. The foundation sponsored the First Annual Iota Black College Tour in 1996 in conjunction with "Positive Black Images," a student group based at City College in San Francisco, and Balboa High School in Maryland. The tour was designed to introduce graduating seniors to historically black colleges and universities. The tour, which included forty seven students and eight staff members, visited the Atlanta University Center, Tuskegee University, and Alabama State University.

The Iota Youth Alliance is a national umbrella program through which individual chapters of Iota Phi Theta address the needs of black youth in their communities. Under the auspices of the Alliance, chapters either work with existing organizations or create new ones based on the requirements and available resources in their locality. In order to ensure continuity, each of the fraternity's chapters is strongly encouraged to give priority to youth alliance activities as part of their program thrust.

The Youth Alliance is important because it allows the fraternity to make a national impact while maintaining ties to those causes and organizations with which it has had historic relationships. An example of Iota Youth Alliance activity is the African American Male Educational Network. It was created and sponsored by the Beta Omega Graduate Chapter in Washington, D.C. AAMEN is a mentoring program for boys between the ages of eight and thirteen. They meet twice a week for tutoring in academic, social and leadership skills.

As a recreational and reinforcement activity, the AAMEN program has formed a Step Team, which performs precision routines that demonstrate the positive principles of AAMEN. Membership on the team is contingent on maintaining a 3.0 grade point average. The team has performed in various locations across the country, including Washington, D.C., Columbus, Ohio, and Chicago.

The fraternity was finally admitted to the National Pan-Hellenic council on November 12, 1996, after several years of lobbying. While some members feel the fraternity might lose the edge that comes from being an outsider to older fraternities, the benefits of being part of the NPHC far outweigh any potential drawbacks. For the first time, Iota Phi Theta has a presence on all college campuses, which should lead to continued growth.

Members of Alpha Kappa Alpha greet Jesse Jackson at a rally in Washington, D.C. Alpha Kappa Alpha is the oldest black sorority in the country, founded in 1908 at Howard University.

4

AKA, Delta, and Other Sororities

A t the turn of the century, society frowned on higher education for a woman. Her place was in the home, raising children and taking care of the husband. For African-American woman, the opportunities for higher education were even more scarce than for others. Odds were high that most African-American women did not even finish high school, let alone go to college.

Ethel Hedgeman Lyle was among the lucky few African-American women to attend college. After her summer break from Howard University in the summer of 1907, the sweet and spontaneous Lyle decided it was time to start an African-American sorority. After all, black men were well on their way to establishing several fraternities.

As word spread of Lyle's efforts, eight other women expressed interest in being part of the new organization. They drafted a constitution, decided on their official name, motto, and colors. Everything was presented to the Howard University administration for recognition.

Within six months—a relatively short time for such a radical step—the first ever sorority for African-American women was born: Alpha Kappa Alpha.

From the beginning, Alpha Kappa Alpha created programs that helped not only the membership but the African-American community as well. The founders were leaders within the YWCA and worked in the campus chapter of the NAACP. When blacks began migrating from the South to the North in great numbers, Alpha Kappa Alpha members worked with the Travelers Aid Society to smooth the transition. Whether it was helping out with the push to get women the right to vote or dressing dolls for needy children at the Freedman's Hospital, Alpha Kappa Alpha members were there.

But the sorority wanted more. In 1921, the sorority created its first national program to commemorate the founding of the sorority through literature, art, and music. It was designed to foster pride in African-American life and culture. While focusing on the African-American community, the sorority also maintained its commitment to the membership. It created a revolving fund for students in financial need, and a fund for students who wanted to study abroad. Together, the programs reward students who exemplify Alpha's commitment to high academic standards.

During the 1930s, Alpha members worked with the Mississippi Health Project, designed to provide schooling and library books to the rural and poor population of Mississippi. It also began a summer school for rural teachers that offered classes in child development, vocational education, and various other studies. Alpha also created a lobbying arm called the National Non-Partisan Council on Public Affairs to influence legislators on issues that affected African Americans.

During World War II, Alpha worked in the war effort through a three-part program of Direct War Services, Complete Victory, and Post War Reconstruction. After the war, Alpha's focus centered on four programs: scholarship, undergraduate housing, health, and social action. In the 1960s and 1970s, Alpha—like all African-American fraternities and sororities—became deeply involved in the civil rights movement. In Alpha's case, it became involved with programs designed to help youth and black businesses, including the Cleveland Jobs Corps Center. The program provided job skills while training undergraduate Alphas how to teach and lead. Alpha, with more than 140,000 members in nearly 900 chapters, continues its legacy of work within the African-American community by working to improve mathematics and science education, establishing a Senior Residence Center for aging Alphas, health advocacy, money management, and basic economic skills.

Although Ersa Poston is one of Alpha Kappa Alpha's "Golden Girls," a label the sorority uses for its fifty-year members, she remembers that she and her girlfriends in college had all originally planned to pledge Delta Sigma Theta, a rival sorority that was formed at Howard by disgruntled Alphas in 1912. But there was quite a bit of blackballing that went on some college campuses. No mater how smart or loyal a candidate was, it was possible for only one girl to ruin one's chances of getting into a particular sorority. One of the Delta girls found out that a boy she liked also liked Poston—effectively ending her Delta ambitions. But Poston, who went on to serve under New York Governor Nelson Rockefeller as the first black cabinet officer in the state's history, and then under President Jimmy Carter as a commissioner of the U.S. Civil Service Commission, said things turned out all right for her in the end by joining Alpha Kappa Alpha.

Many say that among the old-guard women of the black elite, you're either a Delta or an AKA—or you're not in a sorority at all. Among this crowd, there are not many choices. At the undergraduate level, the two sororities often compete for the same candidates. The competition that exists between the AKAs and the Deltas is so widely acknowledged that it is unusual to find a well-educated black woman who remains neutral on the issue. They might make comments like "The Deltas are a great second choice for a girl who can't get into AKA."

Since their inception, the two sororities have attempted to distinguish themselves by comparing the grade point averages and other accomplishments of their student members. Even in its first five years of existence, in an act of pure public relations genius, AKA staked its claim on superior scholarship by establishing an AKA award at Howard University for the female student who achieves the highest grade point average. Ironically, in 1913, a Delta—Eva B. Dykes—won the first AKA prize.

Although it is the second oldest of the sororities, the Deltas are the largest black women's organization in the United States. With about 200,000 members in 850 chapters, they have been a powerful force in politics, as well as in civic and social affairs. Delta can trace its history back to 1912 when five undergraduates at Howard University, unhappy with the direction of the Alpha Kappa Alpha sorority, set off to start their own organization. The rebels wanted to present more of a national perspective and to address the issues of the day, which they felt AKA had not done. They also believed AKA had not done everything possible to become a true sorority rather than a club. They also wanted a new name and symbol to reflect the new identity.

One of the first political acts by the sorority was participating in the 1913 Women's Suffragette March, attended by 10,000 women. It was a daring move by the young sorority because the suffragette movement was not popular at the time. They participated in the march in defiance of the Howard University administration and, in some cases, their own families. Delta women also marched side-by-side (and not in the rear, as had been the custom for black women marchers). It was a proud moment as it foreshadowed the sisters' bold political activism that carries on today.

One of the first programs initiated by Delta was its National Library Project in 1937. It was an attempt to bring literacy to a population whose resources were meager. The Jim Crow laws' "separate but equal" policy systematically provided African Americans with inferior school and library materials. Through the National Library Project, local Delta chapters could help supplement—and in some cases, create—a library for the African-American

The Delta Sigma Theta sorority, founded at Howard University in 1912, has had a long rivalry with Alpha Kappa Alpha. However, while opinions may differ on which is the superior organization, it is a well-known fact that both groups are the top powers among the black sororities.

community. Delta also created one of the country's first book-mobiles, where buses filled with books traveled to different areas of the South to serve isolated communities.

Included in the Delta membership roster through its history have been Patricia Roberts Harris, who served as President Lyndon Johnson's secretary of health, education, and welfare and ambassador to Luxembourg; Senator Carol Mosely-Brown of Illinois; Congresswoman Shirley Chisholm; actress and singer Lena Horne, Mary McLeod Bethune, founder of a college and adviser to First Lady Eleanor Roosevelt; and Dr. Betty Shabazz, wife of Malcolm X.

In addition to organizing their own annual national and regional conferences, the Deltas send delegates to international conferences that address human rights issues. For example, the Deltas sent a team of sisters, including eighteenth national president Hortense Canady, to Beijing, China, for the controversial World Conference on Women. The Delta presented workshops on research and educational issues.

The group has also made presentations at the Congressional Black Caucus' annual legislative weekend. Among the Delta's most prominent members are Dorothy Height and Sadie Alexander. Height, who served as president of the sorority from 1947 until 1958, holds honorary degrees from Tuskegee Institute, Harvard, and many other universities. Her leadership of the National Council of Negro Women and her board membership at the American Red Cross also distinguishes her.

Alexander, the group's first national president, was a Philadelphia attorney and a Ph.D. In 1927 she became the first black woman to graduate from the University of Pennsylvania Law School.

Although they perform a great deal of public service and fundraising to support diabetes research and projects sponsored by the March of Dimes and the National Council of Negro Women, Zeta Phi Beta and Sigma Gamma Rho are not nearly as popular among the old guard. Zeta Phi Beta became the third African-American sorority on the Howard University campus on January 16, 1920. The founders created Zeta's constitution based on their brother organization, Phi Beta Sigma. Thus, Zeta and Sigma became the first and only official Brother and Sister organization.

With a motto of "Scholarship, Service, Sisterhood and Finer Womanhood," Zeta ideals are: furthering the cause of education by encouraging the highest standards of scholarship; uplifting worthwhile projects on college campuses and within communities; and furthering the spirit of sisterly love and promoting the ideals of finer womanhood. In addition to being the first sorority to be officially bound to a fraternity, Zeta can also claim a few other firsts. It was the first sorority to charter chapters in West Africa, Germany, the Bahamas, and St. Croix. It was also the first sorority to form adult and youth auxiliary groups, the Amicae and the Archonettes. Zeta was also the first sorority to organize internal affairs with a national office administered by a paid staff.

Today, Zeta Phi Beta has 85,000 members with 600 chapters around the world. Its membership has included writer Zora Neale Hurston, singer Dionne Warwick, actress Esther Rolle, and former National Bar Association president Algenita Scott Davis.

Some of Zeta's national programs include activities aimed at helping African-American women to become entrepreneurs, to develop relationships with African-American- and female-owned businesses, to assist women in acquiring the skills they need to succeed in the job market, and to encourage women and young girls to pursue careers in space exploration, plumbing, architecture, and contracting, which are not traditionally held by African-American women.

Zeta also sponsors a National Geography Institute, literacy programs, creative arts promotions, conflict resolution and anger management, career and leadership development, governmental affairs, networking, drug and substance abuse prevention programs, and community volunteerism.

The youngest of all the large sororities, Sigma Gamma Rho was founded in 1922 at Butler University in Indianapolis. Its mission was simple: help young African-American women help others through "Greater Service, Greater Progress." So far, about 75,000 members have attempted and succeeded in doing just that.

Author Zora Neale Hurston is one of the more famous sisters of the Zeta Phi Beta sorority, the third African-American sorority to form at Howard University in 1920, and the first to be bound to a fraternity, Phi Beta Sigma.

Being the only African-American sorority founded at a predominantly white institution, the new sorority faced many unique obstacles. In Indiana, the Ku Klux Klan enjoyed a strong base of support. In fact, with more than 30 percent of the male population of the state initiated as members of the KKK, Indiana's nickname during the 1920s was "Klandiana."

It was in this kind of hostile environment that Sigma Gamma Rho not only sought to survive, but also to expand. For the first three years, the sorority did not hold a national convention. Instead, it concentrated on creating a solid foundation for growth in the future.

During the 1930s, Sigma sponsored literary contests that provided books to young African-American students. The sorority chapters also created a Vocational Guidance program that helped young African-American students choose a career path. Another important program, which began during the Great Depression, was the establishment of an Employment Aid Bureau, which helped sisters find new jobs.

Although it has not attracted quite the same number of high-status alumni, Sigma has included Dr. Lorraine Hale, director of Hale House; Congresswoman Corrine Brown of Florida; and Academy Award-winning actress Hattie McDaniel among its members.

W.E.B. DuBois, who cofounded the NAACP, was a member of the Boulé, an organization for professional black men whose official name is Sigma Pi Phi.

5

The Boulé, The Guardsmen, and Other Groups for Men

The first national club established for elite black men was the Boulé, founded in 1904. Its official name is Sigma Pi Phi, but it is not a Greek organization. The Boulé is the quintessential organization for professional black men. Members are not even considered until they have attained a college degree and attended graduate school. It is considered by many to be the elite men's club, and its membership has included the most accomplished, affluent, and influential black men in every city for almost 100 years.

The Boulé distinguishes itself from other clubs for men that might operate only on a local level by selecting its national membership exclusively on the basis of professional accomplishments rather than popularity among a certain local social group. The organization conducts all its official activities and social gatherings in black-tie attire with formal ceremonies. Boulé members are men who are attracted to the fraternity because of its intellectual discussions and its interest in promoting scholarship among a group of accomplished black professional men.

Although the group no longer conducts its activities in secret settings as it did during the first sixty years of existence, it still has strict rules regarding which Boulé events can include nonmembers and which events will exclude unmarried sons and daughters of members. There are even rules regarding the burial or cremation of a deceased member of the Boulé. The group has attorneys, activists, intellectuals, entrepreneurs, socialites, executives, physicians, ambassadors, judges, and politicians, all of them highly accomplished and highly educated.

The group began when Dr. Henry Minton asked five colleagues, all doctors working in Philadelphia, to join him in forming a social organization that would bring together a select group of men with a minimum degree of superior education and culture who were friendly, tolerant, and hospitable. Minton, a graduate of Philips Exeter Academy, the Philadelphia College of Pharmacy, and Jefferson Medical School, was a good example of the kind of black man that the Boulé would both seek and attract. Not only had he been well educated and married into the powerful Wormly family of Washington, D.C., but he was also an achiever who was dedicated to improving the lives of other blacks.

Dr. Minton was responsible for opening the first two hospitals for blacks in Philadelphia—the Mercy and Douglass hospitals. The Mintons who came after him were all dedicated to confronting racial discrimination in Philadelphia. They were constantly talked about for opening doors that previously had been closed to black people.

An intensely intellectual group of men, these six doctors chose to model their group after ancient Greek organizations in terms of structure and nomenclature. The word "boule" was used because it meant "council of noblemen" or "senate." The members were each referred to as "archons," with the president known as the "sire archon." Other officers took Greek titles such as Grammateus, Thesauristes, Rhetoricus, and so forth.

While the 450-page Boulé history book is distributed only to members, most of what it reveals is information that is already open to the public. The gold insignia pins that Boulé members wear on the left side of their crisp white shirts, for example, are given out at a secret ceremony. But the one-inch triangle with Greek letters is visible to any guest who attends a Boulé formal or Boulé funeral, where a deceased member might be buried or cremated with it in accordance with the group's constitution.

Nonmember guests have a general sense that members greet one another with an unusual handshake that is not obvious to others or that they display unusual hand gestures when conducting private meetings. But all of this type of information has remained confidential among the membership. The decision to keep these traditions private was made by the small and introspective first chapter of the group, long before the Boulé became a national organization.

Because the original Philadelphia chapter was slow to expand, subsequent chapters in Chicago, Baltimore, Memphis, and Washington were reluctant to open their membership to men who worked outside the higher education, medical, dental and legal professions. That led to the group quickly being accused of being elitist. But whether it was because they didn't want to dilute their significance by welcoming lesser-known candidates, the members were unapologetic about their decisions to exclude, both then and now. Boulé member Harold Doley, the first black man to own an individual seat on the New York Stock Exchange, said that while some people have used the term "elitist" to describe the club, it was, and still is today, an inaccurate representation.

"It's a little absurd for black people to apologize when they are educated, accomplished, and successful, and to choose to belong to organizations populated with other blacks like them," Doley said.

Like Doley, most of the members in Boulé history have been contributors to, and champions, of black causes. But they do not see their membership in the Boulé as their primary means of contributing to charities or institutions. Doley, who purchased and restored the 20,000-square-foot mansion of the late-nineteenth century black entrepreneur Madam C. J. Walker, has contributed generously to, and sat on the boards of, numerous black colleges, including Shaw University and Clark-Atlanta University.

While many Boulé members have community activities they support, the organization was not created with a social action agenda. It was not designed for community service projects in mind, which is one reason it may not be as well known as the Links, which often hosts highly visible fund-raisers, cotillions, and civic projects.

The membership, about 3,700 in number, is organized into 105 local chapters called "Subordinate Boulés," which represent all the major cities and metropolitan areas where the black elite can be found. In additions to scholars such as W. E. B. DuBois, who earned a Harvard Ph.D. in 1895 and taught at Atlanta University and the University of Pennsylvania, the Boulé can lay claim to dozens of high-profile members, including Dr. Martin Luther King Jr., historian Carter Woodson, Harlem physician Dr. Louis T. Wright, Howard University President James Nabrit, philosopher and Rhodes Scholar Alain Locke, and numerous judges and college presidents.

Among the more recent members are just about every current or former black mayor of a major city, including New York's David Dinkins, Atlanta's Andrew Young and Maynard Jackson, Memphis' Willie Herenton, Baltimore's Kurt Schmoke, Detroit's Dennis Archer, New Orleans' Ernest Morial, Charlotte's Harvey Gantt, and Seattle's Norm Chaneault. Black Enterprise founder Earl Graves, *Essence* magazine founder Ed Lewis, National Urban League heads Whitney Young, Hugh Price, and John Jacob, presidential cabinet secretaries Louis Sullivan, Robert Weaver, Michael Espy and Ron Brown have also been members of the Boulé.

Harold Doley outside of his home, the mansion built by Madam C. J. Walker in 1918. Doley, a Boulé member, was the first black man to own an individual seat on the New York Stock Exchange.

Although some of the old guard complain that getting into the Boulé has become too easy, most would agree that there is no black men's group—fraternal, social or professional—that scrutinizes its candidates more closely. Although it is an unwritten rule, many of the chapters have a tendency to not consider men who are under age sixty five.

While many of the members are lawyers, physicians, dentists, professors, politicians, or business owners, there is no strict professional career requirement that needs to be satisfied in order to be considered for membership. The only requirement is that candidates hold a bachelor's degree or an honorary degree. Traditionally, the selection of members begins as a very quiet nomination process in which the candidate does not even know that he is being considered. There is no application form to fill out. A sponsor quietly collects information about the candidate, in part to avoid embarrassment in case he is rejected.

Many men become members because their father or grand-father belonged. The Boulé is highly aware of the importance of history and family relationships—the Boulé manual and history book lists dozens of father-son memberships, son-in-law member-ships, and family trees displaying generation after generation of blood relations and marital relations that made the prestigious organization a common thread in family history.

Because it is a fraternal group that emphasizes social and intellectual interaction rather than community fund-raising or political activism, there are no public forums or public break-fasts like ones held by the Rotary Club or Kiwanis Club. When money is raised for a charity such as the NAACP or the United Negro College Fund, it is collected directly from members, who simply write a check for the contribution. Many chapters also provide college scholarships and youth development programs that encourage members to mentor local students. Each chapter meets once a month at a private club, restaurant, or conference center that can accommodate the typical thirty-or-more person group.

Membership meetings usually take place monthly on a Thursday, Saturday or Sunday evening, involve a four-course dinner, and include a detailed discussion of a current issue in business, medicine, news, law, or politics that has an impact on black people nationally or abroad. Many Boulé chapters send out reading material to members in advance of the dinner meeting and ask a member who is well informed on the subject to lead the discussion. The monthly meetings, which last three to four hours, are typically for members only, unless an outside speaker is brought in to present an issue. However, the Boulé rarely needs an outside speaker because its members are usually the most interesting and best-connected men among its local membership.

As part of its ongoing evolution, there is one area where members in specific chapters are expressing concern—the area of racial makeup. The Boulé was, of course, started as a fraternity for black men when white clubs were closed to them. There have, however, been a handful of white members who have been asked to join because they were closely associated with some of the high-ranking members, and shared the same liberal views regarding the role and responsibility of black professionals in America. Among the few white members admitted have been Columbia University professor Jack Greenberg, who worked on the 1954 *Brown v. Board of Education* Supreme Court case and who replaced Thurgood Marshall as head of the NAACP Legal Defense Fund after Marshall was named to the federal bench by President John F. Kennedy in 1962. In this respect, the Boulé is more progressive than the black sororities and fraternities, where one finds virtually no white adults in the membership.

As the most selective group for black men in America, the Boulé continues to be popular among both the old guard and the new elite who have earned the traditional academic and professional credentials that the original founders embraced.

Another organization for elite black men is the National Association of Guardsmen. Founded in Brooklyn in 1933, the Guardsmen consists of eighteen chapters scattered throughout the country. Most chapters have fewer than the maximum thirty members allowed, with an emphasis placed on physicians and attorneys. The original Guardsmen included several Brooklyn residents who worked for a downtown oil company.

Jack Greenberg, right, with Thurgood Marshall and James A. Nabrit Jr., is one of the few white men admitted to the Boulé. Greenberg worked on the landmark 1954 case *Brown v. Board of Education* and replaced Marshall as head of the NAACP Legal Defense Fund.

The group is thought of as a purely social organization. Its mandate is very different from that of the more intellectually driven Boulé or the politically active Links group for women, or even the children and family organization, Jack and Jill. Although many Guardsmen have wives in the Links or Girl Friends and children who grew up in Jack and Jill, the group is very clearly an adult men's social club that does not bother with much in the way of formal rules and structures.

While the Boulé's goal has been to gradually increase its size, gain more national stature, and focus its discussions on political and intellectual pursuits, the Guardsmen have chosen to remain small and even more hidden from the public. Most of the early members of the Guardsmen were young lawyers, doctors, and dentists who already belonged to fraternities, according to Theodore Payne, the group's national president in 1997. "I have heard some people describe the Guardsmen as a black man's country club, and I think that description is accurate in some ways," Payne says of the group.

Unlike the Boulé and most other national fraternal groups, the Guardsmen does not have formal conventions with political sessions, platforms, and speeches in a way that the Boulé and fraternities have each year. The organization is so opposed to formalized practices that it allows each chapter to establish its own rules governing dues, how often meetings are held, the number of members permitted, and other important issues. The only strict requirements imposed by the Guardmen are that each chapter serve as a host for the group's scheduled weekend retreats and that each chapter sends at least two delegates to the national gatherings.

Because the group wanted to remain small and elite, it was a long time before the national office would permit creation of chapters west of the Mississippi River. Today, there are chapters in New York, Boston, Baltimore, Atlanta, Detroit, Philadelphia, Chicago, Los Angeles, St. Louis, and Washington, D.C.

The Guardsmen are particularly well known for their lavish "Guardsmen Weekends," where a host chapter offers an all-expenses-paid weekend in the host city for every other Guardsman member and spouse. These weekends take place three times each year and cost host members thousands of dollars for formal dances, golf outings, sightseeing trips, fashion shows and other events. The first weekend takes place in February, March or April; the second in May, June, or July; and the third in September, October, or November. The Guardsmen Weekends scheduling is so important to members that they set the date and location as far as ten years in advance. For example, a recent Guardsmen newsletter has already announced that the Atlanta chapter will be hosting the March weekend in the year 2012.

Besides the extravagant weekends, each chapter holds its own local events. While the different cities do not sponsor cotillions as some of the fraternities do, they do have theme parties and other gatherings. The Los Angeles chapter, for example, throws a lavish New Year's Eve party every year.

Each member of the Guardsmen is given a medallion that has a quill, a winged foot, and helmeted guardsman embossed on it. The group is extremely selective about beginning new chapters and accepting members into the chapters that are already in existence. Because the Guardsmen require a financial outlay greater than all the other men's groups, many eligible men take themselves out of the running because of the expense.

There is no black-tie dinner more coveted among the black elite than those associated with the annual Comus Ball that takes place each year after Christmas in New York.

Each Comus Club member gets only ten invitations to distribute. The group does not sell tickets to the event because they want to act as true hosts. Each member pays for his invited guests. Most members bring their wives, one or two family members, and their very closest friends. Each year, virtually the same crowd attends the dinner and dancing. The groups of people sitting at tables look identical from year to year.

Founded in 1923 in Brooklyn, the Comus Club was started by men who lived and worked in the city, holding a variety of professional and nonprofessional jobs. Unlike the Boulé, whose membership has always been professional, the Comus evolved into a completely professional crowd only after the first couple of decades of its existence. Unlike other black elite groups, the Comus has only one chapter. The club owns a brownstone on Decatur Street in Brooklyn, which members use as a clubhouse where they host Saturday evening meetings, card games, and other affairs. Throughout the 1940s and 1950s, the Comus Club

Christmas ball was held at the Hotel St. George in Brooklyn, but with crowds of 500 or more, it is now held in larger and new facilities like Terrace on the Park in Flushing Meadows or other upscale New York hotels.

Membership in the Comus Club is a much sought-after credential on any black society family résumé. The group is highly selective about admitting new members. Getting any one of the approximately seventy members of the group to reveal anything about the admission process is virtually impossible. In fact, membership seems to be held by many families who pass them between relatives or across generations.

Of all the prominent groups for elite black men, One Hundred Black Men is seen more as a professional organization and less as a selective social club. While some of the most prominent black men in America belong, the group does not have the prestige of a social club because its intent is to serve as a professional networking group. Its chapters are often quite large, and membership is based merely on sponsorship and payment of dues.

Considered a leading force in economic development, mentoring, and networking, One Hundred Black Men was begun in 1963 and now has forty-six chapters around the country. In its early years, the group attracted only its host city's old black family names, but today it has expanded to include young corporate executives, bankers, lawyers, physicians, accountants, entrepreneurs, and politicians. Most chapters have monthly meetings on a selected weekday evening, hosting speakers from the worlds of business or politics, where they discuss practical business strategies, personal improvement, local economic development, or legislation of interest to the black community.

Since members represent some of the most affluent black men in their cities, many of the chapters have established scholarship funds for inner-city young people, or have "adopted" special charitable causes such as a local hospital, a nursing home, a summer camp, the NAACP, or another groups that need their fund-raising support.

Thomas W. Dortch Jr., left, with Detroit mayor Dennis Archer and Atlanta mayor Bill Campbell, is the national president for the One Hundred Black Men organization. Founded in 1963, the group is made up of professional black men but does not have the selectivity of a social club, opting instead to serve as a networking and mentoring group.

One of the founders of One Hundred Black Men was Harvey C. Russell, who was the first black to attain the position of vice president at a Fortune 500 company. As a Pepsi executive in the 1960s, Russell served as a mentor for many young black managers and students who were pursuing careers in corporate America.

"When we started the group there were only 14 or 15 of us, and most of the members were working in local government," said Russell. "Our intent was to create a local networking group for business and political leaders, and we had no idea it would grow into a national organization."

Since forming the first One Hundred Black Men chapter, the New York organization has been particularly successful in its high-profile fund-raising. Talk show host Oprah Winfrey was so impressed with the group's work that she contributed $100,000 to the group's annual black-tie dinner in 1996.

Many One Hundred Black Men members participate in the group because it gives them the opportunity to participate in community service projects that the socially focused groups like the Guardsmen do not participate in on a group level. One Hundred Black men allocates 21 percent of its spending for educational programs and another 13 percent for mentoring programs. Many chapters also operate conflict resolution and antiviolence programs.

Although they have never been as numerous as the women's social groups, several other men's social groups have operated locally or regionally within the black old guard. Among them are the Gallivanters, the Fellas, the Westchester Clubmen, and the Reveille club, all of New York; the Forty Club and the Royal Coterie of Snakes in Chicago; the Rogues of Detroit; the Bachelor-Benedicts in Washington; the Commissioners and the Ramblers of Philadelphia; and the Illinois Club of New Orleans. There are also many men's social groups that are built around specific activities such as boating. New York's Rainbow Yacht Club, which is made up mostly of well-known black physicians who travel in a fleet of yachts during summer weekends.

Some of these groups sponsor important annual events. The Reveille Club, which has been around for almost seventy years, sponsors a "Man of the Year" award. Philadelphia's Ramblers have two annual formals. The Bachelor-Benedicts remain famous because of the debutante cotillion that introduces daughters of some of the city's oldest families.

It was common for women's groups to hold debutante balls for their daughters who were graduating from high school. In addition to these functions, women's groups such as the Links and Girl Friends hold other lavish formal parties and balls.

6

The Links,
Girl Friends,
and Other Groups
for Women

For more than fifty years, membership in the invitation-only Links organization has meant that a black woman's social background, lifestyle, physical appearance, and family's academic and professional accomplishments passed muster with a fiercely competitive group of women who, while forming a rather cohesive sisterhood, are still under each other's constant scrutiny.

Each of nearly 270 local chapters of Links brings together no more than fifty five women. Most of them either professionals, socialites, volunteer fund-raisers, educators, or upper-class matrons. Membership is added only when a current member dies or moves to another city. Although not as old as other elite black women's groups such as the Girl Friends or the National Smart Set, the Links is by far the largest and the most influential. Founded in 1946 by seven well-to-do black women, it contributes millions of dollars to organizations such as the United Negro College Fund and the NAACP Legal Defense Fund. It also supports hundreds of local charities and scholarship programs in the United States and abroad.

A social group with local chapters that meet monthly in members' homes or at restaurants and private clubs, the Links encourages its members to donate more than one million volunteer hours a year and has donated more than $15 million to a wide range of charities and programs in the United States and abroad.

Even while engaging in community affairs, the Links also manages to dominate the social calendars of the black elite with formal parties, annual White Rose balls, debutante cotillions, boat cruises, art auctions, and fashion show luncheons. The stylish women often arrive at larger affairs wearing mink coats, diamonds and pearls, with their husbands helping them from limousines.

The Links' semi-annual conventions are required events for anyone who wants to combine elaborate black-tie dinners with scheduled workshops and debate sessions on such issues as affirmative action, voter registration, national health, or economic development. Following these educational sessions are golf outings, boat rides, and other leisure activities that allow for networking and socializing among members, spouses, and children from around the country.

When Philadelphia natives Sarah Strickland Scott and Margaret Roselle Hawkins conceived of the Links, their plan was to create programs where educated black women could focus attention on civic, educational, and cultural issues. The two women turned to Frances Atkinson, Katie Green, Marion Minton and other women from old-guard Philadelphia families for help in getting the organization started. Their résumés defined the city's black elite.

Scott, who eventually served as the group's first national president, was a perfect example of the well-connected Links member. She was born in 1901 and graduated from the University of Pennsylvania and Columbia University Graduate School. After graduation, she served as a guidance counselor and teacher at schools in Philadelphia and Wilmington, Delaware. Scott's husband, father, and brother were all physicians.

Like Scott, cofounder Hawkins also was a teacher who had graduated from Philadelphia schools. Both had children who were active in the young but growing elite children's group at the time, Jack and Jill.

Whether it was by coincidence or design, the Links group would attract future members from the most stellar backgrounds, or at least members who shared a similar portfolio of social and professional credentials. Patricia Russell McCloud, national president of the Links in 1997 and an attorney in Atlanta, said the organization has always attracted such women, but noted that the group's mission has never included focusing only on social status. "For many years, people wanted to characterize Links members as rich ladies who wore white gloves and sponsored teas and quiet socials," she said. "But we are an activist group that takes on important domestic and international projects that assist blacks, children, and others."

While privileged and professional women make up the vast majority of the Links membership, McCloud said the group's value should be judged by its history of volunteerism and fund-raising and its ability to effect change in the communities it serves.

Of the seven other founding members besides Scott and Hawkins, six were married to doctors. The seventh, Dorothy Wright, was married to Emmanuel Crogman Wright, president of the Citizens and Southern Bank and Trust Company, a black-owned Philadelphia bank. Among the nine Philadelphia women, the most represented church was the extremely patrician St. Thomas Episcopal Church.

The founders of the Links earned degrees from such schools as the University of Pennsylvania, Howard, Hampton, and Temple universities. Most had been active in such groups or institutions as Jack and Jill, the Alpha Kappa Alpha sorority, the NAACP, the League of Women Voters, the Main Line Charity League, the Bryn Mawr School, and the Philadelphia Grand Opera Company.

Soon after its founding, other Links chapters quickly sprung up in Atlantic City, Washington, D.C., St. Louis, Baltimore and New York. There were fifty six chapters by 1952. Although the national office and other Links members closely scrutinize each new chapters and its proposed membership, there are now chapters in such far-flung locations as Beverly Hills, Albuquerque, the Bahamas, and Frankfurt, Germany.

Among the Links' members are some of the most prominent black women in politics, business, education, medicine, and the social world. A look through its membership directory reveals congresswomen Sheila Jackson Lee and Eddie Bernice Jackson of Texas; Children's Defense Fund founder Marian Wright Edelman; Spelman College President Johnetta Cole; former Washington D.C. mayor Sharon Pratt Kelly; the late Betty Shabazz, widow of Malcolm X; former Secretary of Energy Hazel O'Leary; NAACP Legal Defense Fund head Elaine Jones; and numerous philanthropists, college presidents, judges, physicians, bankers, attorneys, corporate executives, and educators, in addition to the wives of such high-profile figures as Congressman Charles Rangel, Vernon Jordan, American Express President Kenneth Chenault, and Harvard psychiatrist Alvin Poussaint.

The Links' annual Easter luncheon and fashion show, known simply as "The Fashion Show," attracts almost 1,000 women each year to the ballroom of either the Waldorf Astoria or the Plaza Hotel in New York City. The women who attend, often attired in fashionable gloves and hats, are almost as well dressed as the models that parade down the ballroom runway. Several publications, including the *New York Times* and the *New York Daily News,* cover the event as a matter of course because of its stature.

Although the local chapters take their direction from the

Elaine Jones of the NAACP, pictured here with Hillary Clinton, is a member of the Links organization. The Links have an impressive list of high-profile members who are involved in politics, business, and other fields.

national office and sponsor similar social events and projects in each city, there are some chapters that have taken on some traditions that are very different from others. The Chicago chapter, for example, is known for the debutante ball it sponsors. The Los Angeles chapter also sponsors a large cotillion. Atlanta has a jazz brunch and San Antonio does many activities with artists and photographers.

What is clearly required of all Links members is the adoption of core program initiatives around the areas of education, health, domestic legislation, international welfare, services for youth, and the arts. The organization's book of program initiatives outlines how chapters can implement certain projects. One idea is to join with the American Cancer Society's National Cancer Initiative mammogram mobile unit and plan mass mammography and examination opportunities for local communities. Another is to encourage Links members to present papers, seminars, and workshops at international conferences with a focus on improving health, education, and housing. Sponsoring voter registration drives, get-out-the-vote carpools, and phone circles are other suggestions.

Because each chapter is limited to fifty five members and new women are often taken in only after a current members gives up her position by death, moving to another city or resignation, admission to the Links is extremely competitive. Unlike sororities, members do not join until well after they have completed college or graduate school. Most join in their forties and fifties, and stay until they die. The admission process is extremely confidential and does not involve a formal application during the initial stages. There is no one to call if you are interested in applying.

Usually, a member who knows the candidate well enough secretly completes an application form detailing personal, academic, and professional characteristics. A significant portion of the application is being able to list family members, related by blood or marriage, who are connected to what they call "Linkdom."

Once the application is passed around to the members for review, a breakfast or luncheon is held where several candidates are auditioned at the same time. They might think they are attending a regular Links activity because there are other guests there as well. But the truth is they are actually auditioned and given a dry run to see how they fit in and interact with the membership. Do they carry themselves well? Are they smart, gracious, interesting? Each of the sponsors is told not to let the candidate know what is going on.

After weeks of reviewing applications and looking over the candidates, the membership votes and either accepts or rejects individual women. If the rules are followed properly, a rejected candidate will never know she has been turned down because she never really knew she was being considered in the first place.

Perhaps more than any other social club, the Links runs itself by a strict code of conduct and will even send senior officials from its national office to mediate certain disputes. Some disagreements, especially over who to admit to the organization, are never discovered by headquarters until it's too late, which is unfortunate.

"This is a wonderful organization but we can all run the risk of getting too caught up in a high-society, club-like mindset," said Anita Lyons Bond, a member of the St. Louis Links. "We need to keep more of our focus on improving the lives of less-advantaged people."

Even though their monthly activities take up a great deal of time and resources, many Links women belong to other groups such as the Girl Friends, the Drifters, or the Northeasterners. Some belong to sororities such as Alpha Kappa Alpha or Delta Sigma Theta. Quite a number are married to men (known as Connecting Links) who are members of the Boulé (Sigma Pi Phi) or the Guardsmen. Naturally, it's common for the children of Links women to be members, or graduates of Jack and Jill.

What the Links boasts in membership numbers and political clout, the Girl Friends can match in social ties and history. Considerably smaller and twenty years older than the Links, the Girl Friends is an organization comprised of stylish black women who are accomplished, well connected and are members of the "Establishment." Most are married to physicians.

The Girl Friends is smaller than the Links because it is even more selective about membership. While the Links used to focus extensively on family background and paid more attention to social status rather than money and clout, the Girl Friends are not interested in that kind of power. It is true that Girl Friends chapters are less likely than the Links to include large number of "power women." But many disagree that the Girl Friends is low-key. Some say that the tight-knit group's claim and emphasis on old-guard families are unparalleled.

Some women, especially those who have been rejected for membership, argue that the Girl Friends is too intimate. Everybody knows everybody's business, they say, because all the women in the group seem to be the daughters of members, the granddaughters of members, or the nieces of members. To some, it almost feels inbred.

While it's difficult to discern which criticisms are legitimate, it is true that the Girl Friends' membership directory offers a surprising amount of personal information on each of its 1,300 members, perhaps supplying more information than any other club directory. The Links directory, for example, lists the name, address, phone number, and spouse's name for each member. The Drifters add the members' birthdays.

The Girl Friends, meanwhile, includes all that information, plus a photograph of the member, the occupation of both the member and her spouse, their children's names, and whether any of their daughters are members. Some also list the professions of their children. One reason for the glut of information is that the families represented by the women in the Girl Friends place great value on tradition and position. Another is that such detail allows people to understand the historic ties between family members and friends.

There is no better representation of this tradition than Phyllis Murphy Stevenson and her mother, Anna Small Murphy. Phyllis was national president of the Girl Friends from 1980 until 1982. Her mother was a charter member when the group was founded in Manhattan in 1927. Anna eventually served as president from 1952 until 1954. Although they are the only mother-daughter team in the organization to hold the title of national president, they are quite similar to other Girl Friends when you look at their ties to other institutions of the black elite. They spent summers in Sag Harbor from the early 1940s when Phyllis was a child. They were both members of Delta Sigma Theta, were educated at Fisk University, and took childhood ballet lessons with Ada Fisher Jones in Harlem. They had a family membership in the Comus Club and friendships with some of the most prominent black families in America.

When the Girl Friends was formed in New York 1927, the intent was to establish a club of young women with similar backgrounds and interests who could meet occasionally for social or intellectual purposes. Most of the founders lived in Harlem, were recent college graduates, or were soon to start graduate school. Most of them had grown up together, attended the same schools or summer camps in upstate New York, or had taken dance or piano lessons together. Since the women who started the club were all quite young, they needed an adult chaperone to go along when they went to public places in New York.

Today, the Girl Friends, Inc. is composed of approximately forty chapters and includes about 1,300 women in cities such as Washington, D.C., Chicago, Pittsburgh, Richmond, Boston, Louisville, Los Angeles, and Atlanta. The club focuses mostly on philanthropic, social, and cultural activities, raising money for local and national charities, as well as sponsoring programs for its own members.

Not to be outdone by their successful husbands, many of the Girl Friends are educators, attorneys, physicians, professors, high profile fund-raisers, and government officials. One example is former Clinton cabinet member Hazel O'Leary, who served as U.S. secretary of Energy. She became a member of the Minneapolis chapter many years after her mother Mattie Ross Reid helped establish the Newport News, Virginia, chapter in 1938. United State Congresswoman Eddie Bernice Johnson belongs to the Dallas, Texas, chapter.

Getting into the Girl Friends is even harder than getting into the Links, except for the daughter of a member. The chapters are usually small (between twenty and thirty members) and no city has more than one chapter. It takes a wave of resignations or deaths to improve the chances of being accepted. There is no application to fill out and no membership office to call. Two members must sponsor candidates and two-thirds of the membership must vote in favor to be admitted. If a woman is turned down, that chapter can never propose her again.

In addition to the charity work, the Girl Friends for many years has been known for its debutante cotillions, where high school seniors are presented at downtown hotels or country clubs accompanied by their fathers and young escorts dressed in tuxedos. The Ball of Roses cotillion was adopted by other chapters but originated with the New York chapter. The event is held around Christmas at the Waldorf Astoria on Park Avenue in New York City. Each debutante is selected through a rigorous process that compares applicants' college plans, career goals, and accomplishments.

While some chapters have abandoned cotillions because of their association with elitist activities, the group continues to publish its annual journal *Chatterbox*, which looks and reads like a black version of *Town & Country* magazine. Each chapter's activities of the year are highlighted and illustrated with photographs from formal parties, outdoor picnics, and other organized activities.

Members and their families are captured in photographs at college graduations, battleship launchings, judicial swearing-in ceremonies, political campaign speeches, White House dinners and other interesting events. New York artist Romare Beardon designed the cover to the May 1952 *Chatterbox* as a tribute to his mother's ties to the group.

Another popular group for black women is the Drifters. It is smaller and less driven by family heritage than the Girl Friends. The Drifters consists of about thirty chapters across the country, with groups kept to a maximum of twenty members. Their focus

Former Secretary of Energy Hazel O'Leary is a member of the Links and the Girl Friends. Her mother was one of the founders of the Girl Friends' Newport News, Virginia, chapter. Membership in the Girl Friends is usually difficult unless one is the daughter of a member.

is on charitable work, such as sponsoring scholarships for students going away to college. The Drifters began in 1954 simultaneously in Waco, Texas, and Chicago. The 500-member group has a high percentage of academics, attorneys, and other professionals. Unlike the Girl Friends, the Drifters are inclined to organize frequent extravagant vacation trips for their members and friends. They travel to such locales as Haiti, St. Martin, Greece, and Africa.

Each August, the Drifters chapters come together for a national conference and announce the names of graduating high school seniors from each chapter who will receive a college scholarship. Since 1969 the Drifters have also maintained a noninterest-bearing loan fund to assist students attending targeted colleges. Among the schools on the list are Bennett College, LeMoyne-Owen College, Bethune-Cookman College, Howard University School of Nursing, and Virginia Union University.

Another active group for black women is the Northeasterners, founded in the early 1930s. There are twelve chapters, most with no more than twenty members each. When it comes to social activities, the Northeasterners do not sell tickets to its formal dances, as the Links and other organizations do. They have a small number of guests and members pay for everything. Three sisters founded the Northeasterners in 1921 in New Haven, Connecticut. The group grew slowly and formed chapters in Pittsburgh, Philadelphia, Washington, Chicago, Indianapolis, and other cities were blacks were concentrated.

Like the Drifters and the Northeasterners, the National Smart Set is a moderate-sized women's group with a fairly prestigious roster of female members. It was founded in 1937 by a group of Washington, D.C.-area schoolgirls who were going off to college at Howard University. The Smart Set is more like the Girl Friends than the Links because of its focus on social events. The group sponsors three major black-tie social events each year, as well as an outdoor summer activity at a member's residence. Because the Smart Set has not become as large as some other organizations, its members remain intimate and keep up with each other's activities through the organization's fun and gossipy *Smart Set Talk* magazine. The publication reports on contributions given to the NAACP as well as more personal events in members' lives.

Founded in 1956 by a group of women from Philadelphia, Baltimore, Newport News, and Washington, D.C., the Continental

Societies, Inc. is another popular club among black women. It has 465 chapters in most American cities and Bermuda. The Continentals provide programs and raise money for young people, families, and institutions that focus on health, employment, recreation, and education.

Another group that had the potential of being an important national group but resisted spreading beyond its charter city was the Hillbillies. It was created by a group of young women who lived in Sugar Hill, the most exclusive section of northern Harlem, in the 1930s. Still another rather small group for African-American women is the Carats, first formed in the mid-1970s. Its 300 members belong to chapters in thirteen cities, including Cleveland, New York, Detroit, and Macon, Georgia. In addition to hosting social functions, the group awards scholarships to college students.

Attendees of the exclusive Negro Ball in 1935 in New York. The issue of a black upper class is a troublesome one, for both blacks and whites. The mere existence of such a class presents a much more complex picture of the African-American community, which some feel does not help the cause of racial equality.

7

A Complex
Community

The organizations discussed here are a sensitive subject for some in the African-American community. The idea of elitism to exist within an ethnic group that has struggled for equality throughout the twentieth century can be troublesome. Some fear it may set back the African-American cause. As Graham notes, "Some have argued that the mere discussion of class differences within the black community serves to undermine the possibility of unifying a race that has long faced other serious challenges." Conversely, he writes, "Many others would insist that to disregard class differences among black Americans would be to treat the population as a monolith—a group with only one experience and one perspective."

African Americans can find themselves to be burdened with the threat of "sellout" accusations should they actually succeed and find financial success. One common complaint of the successful television series *The Cosby Show* was that it didn't accurately reflect the lives of "most" African Americans, as the Huxtable family were affluent (Dr. Huxtable was an obstetrician while Mrs. Huxtable was a lawyer) and lived in an upscale neighborhood, instead of the projects or other settings that American television audiences were accustomed to seeing.

However, one can view the Huxtable family on *The Cosby Show* as an allegory for the existence of these civic orgnizations and groups such as the Boulé or Jack and Jill. These successful blacks could serve as role models for others to show that it is indeed possible to be an African American and attain financial wealth and/or political power, things that need not merely be associated with whites. Indeed, their mere existence can counter racial stereotypes and show that the African-American lobby can be powerful and influential itself.

Naturally, it is a tricky balance to achieve. Given some of these organizations' reliance on connections and/or family legacies in recruiting, some might resent the insular and seemingly elitist nature of their membership policies. They may see no difference between the inaccessibility of the white upper class and that of the black upper class. Even those who may not have old-money connections may find acceptance to be elusive in certain parts of the country, which Graham discovered upon asking his friend about the idea of Graham's brother moving to Atlanta from New York:

> One childhood friend, who had relocated to Atlanta after practicing medicine in New York, told us, "You can make a million dollars a year and live in the nicest house in Buckhead [a prestigious section in Atlanta], but you'll never be accepted by the old black elite in this town."
>
> "These people will stare you in the face after you've told them of your great accomplishments," explained our friend, "and the only thing that will matter to them is who in your family went to

Morehouse, and for how many generations your family has lived in Atlanta."

This was not the only opinion we heard of the old-guard blacks in the city, but we heard enough similar stories to convince us that my brother should reconsider his plans and remain in New York, where family lineage mattered less.

Beyond the conflict between such entrenched traditions as family background, there is another strange issue among members of the African-American elite—that of skin color. Even at a young age, Graham was all too aware of the connotations of lighter skin versus darker. His grandmother would discourage him from even associating with darker-skinned children, as well as admonish them for staying too long in the sun lest they get darker.

The "brown paper bag and ruler test" compared skin tones to that of a brown paper bag, and the straightness of hair to a ruler. Those who passed this test would be considered more attractive, though the skin tone and hair quality would also carry a stigma of a background that might not be so well to do. But complicating this issue is the ramifications of the origins of such physical characteristics. Graham explains that many light-skinned blacks were mulattoes who were descendants of slaveowners. Even though they were still considered slaves, these lighter-skinned blacks were given special treatment over their fieldhand brethren, often working in the slaveowner's house.

The black elite will have to continue to grapple with the issue of either using one's prestigious family background or one's working-class roots as a point of pride, without having to apologize for either. But it is telling that they do experience the same backlash that many well-to-do whites do with regard to class and power. Perhaps no one is ready to admit yet that the African-American community is far more complex and conflicted than it appears. But hopefully, its members will be able to resolve its various differences and be able to take pride no matter what their background, and be able to work together for a common cause. As Graham himself writes,

> Making the climb from slavery and blatant discrimination to wealth and achievement is what the promise of America is supposed to be about. The families of the black elite embody the best of the American dream. For this reason, the story of the black upper class is a story of America.

1904 The Boulé is founded.

1906 Alpha Phi Alpha fraternity is founded.

1907 Alpha Kappa Alpha sorority is founded.

1911 **May 15** Kappa Alpha Nu fraternity is founded.

Nov. 17 Omega Phi Psi fraternity is founded.

1912 Delta Sigma Theta sorority is founded.

1913 Phi Beta Sigma fraternity is founded.

1914 Kappa Alpha Nu changes its name to Kappa Alpha Psi.

Phi Beta Sigma fraternity is founded.

1920 Zeta Phi Beta sorority is founded.

1921 The Northeasterners is founded.

1923 The Comus Club is founded.

1927 The Girl Friends is founded.

1933 The National Association of Guardsmen is founded.

1937 The National Smart Set is founded.

1938 First meeting of Jack and Jill of America, Inc.

1946 The Links is founded.

1954 The Drifters is founded.

1956 The Continental Societies is founded.

1963 Iota Phi Theta fraternity is founded.

One Hundred Black Men is founded.

1968 Jack and Jill of America Foundation, Inc. is founded.

1981 Kappa Alpha Psi Foundation is founded.

Graham, Lawrence Otis. *Our Kind of People: Inside America's Black Upper Class.*
New York: HarperCollins, 1999.

Ross, Lawrence C. Jr. *The Divine Nine: The History of African American
Fraternities and Sororities.* New York: Kensington Publishing Corp., 2000.

"Climbing New Hills," *Ebony,* October 1997. Vol. 52, p. 44.

Bauchum, Rosalind G. "African American Organizations, 1794-1999." Roman and Littlefield, January 2002.

Boyer, Karl P. "Positive and Black: A Resource Directory of Famous Contemporary African Americans and Organizations," *Black&Postive*. September 1993.

Graham, Lawrence Otis. *Our Kind of People: Inside America's Black Upper Class.* New York: HarperCollins, 1999.

Knupfer, Anne Meis. *Toward a Tenderer Humanity and a Nobler Womanhood: African American Women's Clubs in Turn-Of-The-Century Chicago.* New York: New York University Press, 1996.

http://www.apa1906.org
Alpha Phi Alpha Fraternity

http://www.iotaphitheta.org
Iota Phi Theta Fraternity

http://www.kapsi.org
Kappa Alpha Psi Fraternity

http://www.omegapsiphifraternity.org
Omega Psi Phi Fraternity

http://www.pbs1914.org
Phi Beta Sigma Fraternity

http://www.aka1908.org
Alpha Kappa Alpha Sorority

http://www.dst1913.org
Delta Sigma Theta Sorority

http://www.sgr1922.org
Sigma Gamma Rho Sorority

http://www.zpb1920.org
Zeta Phi Beta Sorority

http://www.jack-and-jill.org
Jack and Jill of America, Inc.

■ ■ ■ **ABOUT THE AUTHOR**

Joe Ferry is a veteran journalist who has worked for several newspapers in the Philadelphia area since 1977. He is a graduate of West Catholic High School for Boys in Philadelphia and Eastern College in St. Davids, PA. Mr. Ferry has also written about actor/director Rob Reiner and actress Helen Hunt for Chelsea House. He lives in Perkasie, Bucks County, Pennsylvania with his wife, three children, and two dogs.